Lemon
1/N 09428
w 323672
$30

THREAT TO THE GIANT PANDA

John A. Torres

Mitchell Lane
PUBLISHERS

P.O. Box 196
Hockessin, Delaware 19707
Visit us on the web: www.mitchelllane.com
Comments? email us: mitchelllane@mitchelllane.com

Mitchell Lane
PUBLISHERS

Printing   1   2   3   4   5   6   7   8   9

A Robbie Reader/On the Verge of Extinction: Crisis in the Environment

Frogs in Danger
Polar Bears on the Hudson Bay
The Snows of Kilimanjaro
Threat to Ancient Egyptian Treasures
Threat to Haiti
Threat to the Bengal Tiger

Threat to the Giant Panda
Threat to the Leatherback Turtle
Threat to the Monarch Butterfly
Threat to the Spotted Owl
Threat to the Whooping Crane
Threat to the Yangtze River Dolphin

Library of Congress Cataloging-in-Publication Data
Torres, John.
  Threat to the giant panda / by John Torres.
     p. cm. — (On the verge of extinction. Crisis in the environment)
  "A Robbie Reader."
  Includes bibliographical references and index.
  ISBN 978-1-58415-689-5 (library bound : alk. paper)
  1. Giant panda—Juvenile literature. 2. Endangered species—Juvenile literature. 3. Giant panda—Conservation—Juvenile literature. I. Title.
  QL737.C27T67 2009
  333.95'9789—dc22
                                                                    2008020894

ABOUT THE AUTHOR: John A. Torres is an award-winning newspaper reporter from Central Florida. His stories have taken him to Africa, Italy, Indonesia, Mexico, India, and Haiti. He has covered natural disasters, Olympic sporting events, the AIDS pandemic in Africa, and even spent a week in a drug-infested neighborhood in 2007 to write a series of articles about the community.

Torres is the author of more than 40 children's books, ranging from sports and entertainment to environmental threats and natural disasters. He has written many titles for Mitchell Lane Publishers, including *Meet Our New Student from Haiti; Threat to Haiti; Hurricane Katrina and the Devastation of New Orleans, 2005; Disaster in the Indian Ocean, Tsunami, 2004;* and *The Ancient Mystery of Easter Island.*

PUBLISHER'S NOTE: The facts on which this story is based have been thoroughly researched. While every possible effort has been made to ensure accuracy, the publisher will not assume liability for damages caused by inaccuracies in the data, and makes no warranty on the accuracy of the information contained herein.
                                                                    PLB

TABLE OF CONTENTS

Words in **bold** type can be found in the glossary.

EXTINCTION

According to a Chinese legend, pandas were completely white until one cub had a frightening experience with a leopard.

A LEGEND IS BORN

As the leopard circled, the young shepherdess gathered her sheep and the little white bear who played with them. Waving a stick, she tried to scare the leopard away—but it was too late. The cat pounced. To save the cub, the girl jumped in front of the leopard and was killed.

News of this **heroic** (heh-ROH-ik) deed spread fast, and white bears from all over the land came to the girl's funeral to honor her. To show how sad they were, the bears wore black bands on their arms.

They spoke about how the young girl had saved the cub from the leopard, and they cried. They wiped their tears, making the

Leopards are the panda's only natural enemy. Like the panda, the leopard is losing its habitat in China, and its range is getting smaller.

black ink on their armbands run. As they hugged one another, they spread the ink to other bears.

They decided to leave the marks on their bodies to remember the little girl who gave her life for them. They thought their babies should have the marks as well. These white Chinese bear-cats, as they were once called, were now black-and-white pandas.

This **legend** explains why pandas look the way they do. No one knows where the legend began, but the story takes place in Wolong Valley in China, where the giant panda still lives. There are many different versions of the legend.

No one in the West had ever even heard of the giant panda until 1869, when French **missionary** (MIH-shuh-nayr-ee) Armand David was given the skin of a giant panda. Later, the Field Museum of Natural History in Chicago hired hunters to shoot one and bring it back to the museum. About fifty years later, Americans began to fall in love with the cuddly-looking creatures.

Armand David traveled to China to teach people about his religion. He became interested in the plants and animals there, and collected many samples for French scientists.

A panda cub explores its surroundings near its mother. Cubs stay with their mothers until they are two years old.

In panda reserves, the bears live in groups. In the wild, however, pandas are solitary animals.

These bears are usually the most popular animal in the zoo. Although people love them, the bears are **endangered** (en-DAYN-jerd).

By 2008, **conservationists** (kon-sir-VAY-shuh-nists) and scientists estimated there were only between 1,500 and 3,000 pandas living in the wild. If something were not done to preserve their **environment** (en-VYE-urn-ment) and to help save them, the giant panda would become extinct.

EXTINCTION

At the Smithsonian National Zoological Park in Washington, D.C., Tian Tian sits and nibbles on a piece of bamboo. Giant pandas have large flat teeth called molars and strong facial muscles for grinding tough bamboo stems.

Chapter Two **2**

A CHINESE BEAR

Giant pandas are found in the wild in only one country in the world: China. They live in a few small mountain ranges in central China, in the Sichuan, Shaanxi, and Gansu provinces. Before the giant panda was endangered, many pandas lived in lowland forest areas. As more people moved to those areas, and as they cleared the land to farm, the giant pandas moved to higher ground in the mountains. Now they sometimes live as high as the clouds. Their thick fur is perfectly adapted for life in these cold areas of heavy rain and mist.

Giant pandas spend most of the day **foraging** (FOR-uh-jing) for food, which is 99 percent bamboo leaves and stalks. In

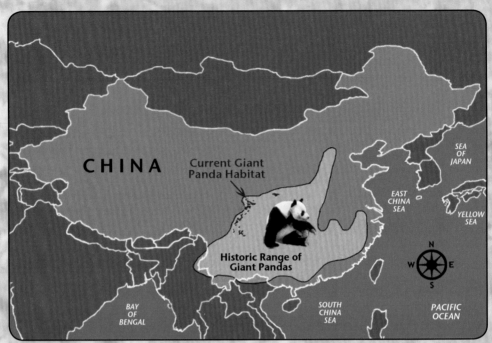

Giant pandas once roamed southern China, but they are now confined to isolated patches (in red) on six mountain ranges.

order to stay healthy, they need to eat up to 40 pounds of bamboo every day. Once in a while they will also eat other types of plants and even small rodents.

Although these bears are called "giant," they are not really gigantic at all. They are about the same size as their American cousins, the black bear—about four feet tall when walking on all fours. When pandas stand up, they are about six feet tall. A full-grown adult weighs about 250 pounds. By comparison, Alaska's Kodiak bears can stand up to 10 feet tall and can weigh more than 1,000 pounds.

Kodiak bears, which live in Alaska, are much larger than the "giant" panda. While pandas eat mostly bamboo, Kodiak bears eat a lot of salmon, a type of fish.

In the wild, giant pandas live mainly **solitary** lives, meaning they live alone most of the time. Pandas start mating when they reach about four years old. Usually the mating season takes place between March and May. The mother panda is the only one who takes care of the baby. Usually two panda cubs are born, but since the mother can care for only one, she abandons the other.

The panda cub can start eating bamboo when it is six months old. By the time it is two years old, it leaves its mother and goes off on its own.

Tai Shan, who was born at the Smithsonian's National Zoo in Washington, D.C., plays in the snow with his mother, Mei Xiang. Most bears hibernate when the weather gets too cold. Pandas do not hibernate. In winter, they just move to a warmer area.

Pandas are happy on the ground and in trees. They use their long claws to help them climb.

Because they live mainly in colder climates, pandas are one of the few bears that do not **hibernate** (HYE-bur-nayt), or sleep through the winter in a cave or den. Leopards are the only natural enemy of the giant panda, but they will attack only the cubs, and not a full-grown bear.

People love giant pandas. Maybe it's because of the way they look, or because they sit upright when they eat, or because they look cuddly. If they are so popular, then why are they in danger of becoming extinct?

EXTINCTION

A wild panda forages for food in the mountains of China. Although they look cuddly, pandas, like other bears, can be dangerous. They will attack humans if they get angry.

Chapter Three 3

ENDANGERED

Giant pandas have been considered rare since the 1960s. In 1990, the International Union for Conservation of Nature (IUCN) placed the bear on its endangered species list. When a species is placed on this list, the world begins taking steps to protect it from **extinction** in the wild.

There are several reasons for the falling numbers of wild giant pandas, but the main reason is loss of habitat—which includes bamboo. Giant pandas spend most of their day searching for and eating bamboo, which normally grows in forests in the shade of tall trees. People have been cutting down these trees for logging and to make room for

Bamboo is a kind of grass. There are many types of bamboo, some of which can grow to 100 feet tall. It is also one of the fastest-growing plants. Some types can grow more than one foot a day. However, there are fewer places for bamboo to grow than there used to be.

farming and building houses. The Chinese government no longer allows logging where giant pandas live, but sometimes people clear the land anyway.

It is also illegal to hunt giant pandas. However, when giant pandas have to travel far to find food, they sometimes get caught in traps that are set for other animals. Other pandas are **poached**, or hunted illegally for their fur.

The Chinese government has started stepping up law **enforcement** (en-FORS-ment) efforts. Police checkpoints on giant panda reserves make sure people are not cutting down trees or hunting the animal. Police officers inspect all cars that pass the checkpoints.

The skeleton of a panda on display at the Museum of Natural History in London, England. Scientists can better learn how to protect the panda by studying its habits as well as its bones.

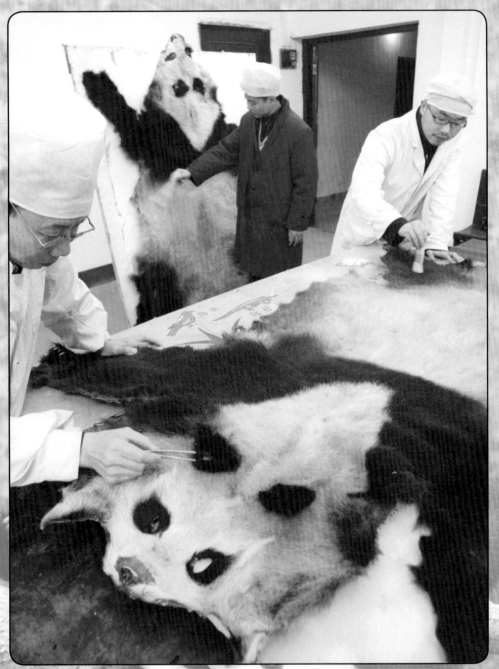

Specialists repair panda furs at the Chongqing Nature Museum. China has come down hard on poachers—people who kill pandas for their fur. The poachers who killed these two pandas were arrested.

Another major problem is called **fragmentation** (frag-men-TAY-shun). This is when humans divide the land so much that animals become separated from one another. Since giant pandas live alone most of the time, they sometimes have to travel far to find a mate. These animals are so shy that they will not cross an area where there is a village or even power lines. Female giant pandas mate only once a year, and they are **fertile** for only a few days. When it is time to have cubs, it is vital that the animals be able to find each other.

If nothing is done to save the giant panda's habitat, or to ensure that they can get together to mate, then surely this rare animal will die out.

EXTINCTION

Mei Xiang licks her cub, Tai Shan, as the five-month-old explores his outdoor play area. She will keep a close eye on him as he climbs around and tests his strength. China has loaned Mei Xiang and other pandas to the United States to help raise awareness and money for these endangered animals.

Chapter Four **4**

A SIMPLE SOLUTION?

The Chinese government started giant panda conservation efforts in the late 1940s, but it wasn't until the 1970s that it began taking serious steps to save these animals. There are also many private groups that are dedicated to saving the giant panda from extinction. These groups agree that one of the best solutions is quite simple—education. They feel that the more the world knows about giant pandas, the more people will do to save the animals. With more study, they believe, they can more easily find out what must be done to save them.

Giant pandas do not stand a chance unless their habitat remains protected. By

2008, there were about 50 giant panda reserves, or protected areas, in China. These areas also protect red pandas, golden monkeys, and other endangered animals.

In May 2008, a severe earthquake that killed thousands of people in China also affected many giant pandas, including those at the Wolong Nature Reserve. Much of their habitat was destroyed, and eight of the

Red pandas look like a cross between a raccoon and a fox. They are not related to the giant panda, but they do eat a lot of bamboo.

Chinese soldiers carry a giant panda off the Wolong Nature Reserve to safety after a massive earthquake struck China in May 2008.

dozens of giant pandas that lived there had to be moved to a zoo. The reserve's workers were also able to rescue the cubs.

Another program for protecting the giant panda is called captive breeding and reintroduction (ree-in-troh-DUK-shun). Scientists in zoos and research centers are helping the animals breed and raise their cubs. Then, when the cubs are old enough and have been taught survival skills, they are

Tai Shan, a panda cub, was born on July 9, 2005, at the Smithsonian National Zoological Park in Washington, D.C.

August 2—Tai Shan's first health exam. He weighs 1.82 pounds and measures 12 inches long.

September 19—Tai Shan's sixth health exam. He weighs 9.57 pounds and measures 22.51 inches.

October 21—Tai Shan's ninth exam. He weighs 14.1 pounds and is 27.1 inches long.

November 21—Tai Shan, with his mom, is four months old, weighs 19.2 pounds, and is 31.2 inches.

December 22—Tai Shan is five months old. He gets to go outside for the first time.

July 9, 2006—Tai Shan enjoys his frozen fruit and vegetable treat on his first birthday.

set free (or reintroduced) into the wild.

Giant panda coin

Raising money for panda reserves is an important step in saving the panda. Many wildlife groups raise money for research, to buy special equipment and food, and to help pay for animal doctors at the reserves in China. When people go to a zoo and look at the giant pandas, they are helping to raise money for panda research and conservation.

The world may finally be realizing how important it is to protect an animal species that is nearing extinction. While the future of the giant panda is still not very bright, experts say that the number of giant pandas in the wild is no longer going down and may even be going up little by little. With continued support, the giant panda may be saved from extinction.

WHAT YOU CAN DO

With your help, the giant panda may roam the forests of China for a long time to come. Here are a few things you can do.

Read more books about the giant panda, and visit Internet sites dedicated to saving these animals. Tell your friends about giant pandas and why it's important to save them. Visit a zoo that features pandas.

Research how you can "adopt" a panda. Check out the Wildlife Adoption Center at the Defenders of Wildlife web site for more information: https://secure.defenders.org/site/SPageServer?pagenam e=wildadopt_panda&s_src=WJY08WDADOPT&s_ subsrc=WJY08WDADOPT_factsheet

You can also write letters to wildlife organizations and to politicians urging them to continue conservation efforts for the giant panda. Find your U.S. Representative at https://forms.house.gov/wyr/welcome.shtml

Some organizations that work to help giant pandas:

Defenders of Wildlife
National Headquarters
1130 17th Street, NW
Washington, DC 20036
(800) 385-9712
http://www.panda.org/how_you_
can_help/

Friends of the National Zoo (FONZ)
P.O. Box 37012 MRC 5516
Washington, DC 20013-7012
(202) 633-3034
http://nationalzoo.si.edu/JoinFONZ/
Join/

World Wildlife Fund
U.S. Headquarters
1250 Twenty-Fourth Street, N.W.
P.O. Box 97180
Washington, DC 20090-7180
(202) 293-4800
http://www.worldwildlife.org/
species/finder/giantpanda/item565.
html

Books

Amato, Carol A. *The Giant Panda: Hope for Tomorrow.* Illustrated by David Wenzel. Hauppauge, New York: Barron's Educational Series, 2000.

Claybourne, Anna. *Giant Panda: In Danger of Extinction! (Animals Under Threat).* Portsmouth, New Hampshire: Heinemann, 2005.

Granfield, Linda. *The Legend of the Panda.* Illustrated by Song Nan Zhang. Toronto, Canada: Tundra Books, 2001.

Maple, Terry L. *Saving the Giant Panda.* Atlanta, Georgia: Longstreet Press, 2001.

Seidensticker, John, and Susan Lumpkin. *Giant Pandas.* New York: Harper Collins, 2007.

Works Consulted

Bodeen, Christopher. "Death Toll in China Earthquake Up to Nearly 9,000." *Associated Press.* May 12, 2005. http://www.comcast.net/articles/news-general/20080512/China.Earthquake/

Branigan, Tania. "Hugs for Pandas Shocked by Quake." *The Guardian.* June 3, 2008. http://www.guardian.co.uk/world/2008/jun/03/chinaearthquake.wildlife

Grinberg, Emanuella. "China's Giant Pandas Survive Earthquake." *CNN.* May 13, 2008. http://www.cnn.com/2008/WORLD/asiapcf/05/13/china.pandas/

"Missing Panda Seized after Sichuan Earthquake." May 26, 2008. http://www.chinadaily.com.cn/china/2008-05/26/content_6712647.htm

Smithsonian National Zoo Panda Cub. http://newsdesk.si.edu/photos/nzp_panda_cub.htm

On the Internet
Defenders of Wildlife
http://live.defenders.org/wildlife_and_habitat/wildlife/
panda.php
Giant Panda Survival Plan
http://www.giantpandaonline.org
Panda Channel
http://now.com.hk/panda/
Pandas International's (Save the Pandas) Annual Report
http://www.pandasinternational.org
Smithsonian National Zoological Park
http://nationalzoo.si.edu/Animals/GiantPandas
Wolong Panda Club
http://www.pandaclub.net/
World Wildlife Fund: Giant Panda
http://www.worldwildlife.org/species/finder/giantpanda/
item565.html

PHOTO CREDITS: Cover, pp. 1, 3 (background), 18—JupiterImages; pp. 4, 22, 26 (top, right; bottom, left)—Jessie Cohen/
Smithsonian National Zoo; pp. 5-32 background, 14, 15, 26 (bottom, right)—Ann Batdorf/Smithsonian National Zoological Park; pp.
8, 24, 26—Smithsonian National Zoological Park; p. 10—Jeff Kubina/Smithsonian National Zoological Park; p. 12—Sharon Beck; p.
19—Barbara Marvis; p. 20—AP Photo/EyePress; p. 25—Loi Jin/AFP/Getty Images.

conservationists (kon-sir-VAY-shuh-nists)—People who work to save the environment.

endangered (en-DAYN-jerd)—In need of protection to avoid becoming extinct.

enforcement (en-FORS-munt)—Actions that help make sure people obey the laws.

environment (en-VYE-urn-ment)—A person's or animal's surroundings.

extinction (ek-STINK-shun)—The dying out of an entire type of plant or animal.

facial (FAY-shul)—Of the face.

fertile (FER-tul)—Physically prepared to mate.

foraging (FOR-uh-jing)—Searching the wilderness for food.

fragmentation (frag-men-TAY-shun)—Becoming divided into very small pieces.

heroic (heh-ROH-ik)—Brave.

hibernate (HYE-bur-nayt)—To spend the winter in a deep sleep.

legend (LEH-jund)—A story that has been told many times, and that cannot be confirmed as fact.

missionary (MIH-shuh-nayr-ee)—A person who travels to help others and to spread the religion of Christianity.

poached—Hunted game or fish illegally.

solitary (SAH-lih-tar-ee)—Alone.